Life Maximizers

by
Dr. Ron Jenson

HONOR
BOOKS

Tulsa, Oklahoma

Life Maximizers
ISBN 1-56292-158-4
Copyright © 1997 by Dr. Ron Jenson

Published by Honor Books
P.O. Box 55388
Tulsa, Oklahoma 74155

INTRODUCTION

You are moving toward your concept of success, but is it the right concept?

Your concept of success has been developed and conditioned over the years by the media, your family, your peers, your associates, and your experiences — the net effect of these may be positive or negative. You may be under the impression that success is power, prosperity, position, prestige, and pleasure. While it may include these, it really involves much more.

Success is achievement and fulfillment in all areas of life, while having a significant, positive impact on those around you. If you succeed in work alone and fail in personal relationships, you're not succeeding. If you accomplish great things, but live miserably in the process, you're not succeeding — you're not maximizing your life!

Being a life maximizer is the progressive realization of **all** *that you were meant to be and do.* But how do you maximize your life?

First, it all depends on what you do with you, the way you manage yourself. Second, the way you manage yourself is only as good as the principles or universal truths upon which you build your life. Only a life rooted in real and lasting values is successful in all areas. Just as there are physical laws that govern the physical universe, so there are universal principles that govern our existence. These principles are abiding truths — absolute and non-negotiable. They are as factual as the law of gravity.

Life Maximizers outlines these principles, which can be found in the word, "M-A-X-I-M-I-Z-E-R-S." The following two pages contain the Maximizer Principles and the Maximizer's Creed; then each section contains thought-provoking reminders to apply these principles in your own life.

Truth is the source of authentic success. If you really want to win in life, you must passionately pursue the discovery of truth and learn how to apply that truth appropriately, which is wisdom.

So turn the page — if you dare — and begin to maximize your life!

(Note: Except where indicated all quotes are by Ron Jenson.)

MAXIMIZERS

Make things happen.

Achieve personal significance.

X out the negatives.

Internalize right principles.

March to a mission.

Integrate all of life.

Zero in on caring for people.

Energize inner life.

Revise actions rigorously.

Stay the course.

MAXIMIZER'S CREED

I will take charge of my life and be a difference-maker.

I will live my life with a sense of destiny.

I will embrace problems as positive opportunities.

I will center my life on bedrock principles.

I will passionately pursue my mission.

I will keep all vital areas of my life in balance.

I will put others first and honestly serve them.

I will cultivate my character and spirit.

I will keep adjusting to needs.

I will never, ever, ever quit.

MAKE THINGS HAPPEN.

I WILL TAKE CHARGE OF MY LIFE
AND BE A DIFFERENCE-MAKER.

THE BEST YEARS OF YOUR LIFE ARE THE
ONES IN WHICH YOU DECIDE YOUR
PROBLEMS ARE YOUR OWN. YOU DON'T
BLAME THEM ON YOUR MOTHER, THE
ECOLOGY, OR THE PRESIDENT. YOU
REALIZE THAT YOU CONTROL YOUR
OWN DESTINY.

— ALBERT ELLIS

YOUR DECISION TO
TAKE CHARGE OF YOUR LIFE —
THAT IS THE SEED OF SUCCESS.

IT ISN'T ENOUGH TO BE BUSY. ANTS ARE
BUSY. THE QUESTION IS, WHY ARE YOU
BUSY? WHAT ARE YOU ACCOMPLISHING?
WHAT ARE THE RESULTS YOU'RE
LOOKING FOR? YOU NEED TO BE
CONSCIOUS OF THESE THINGS.

— HENRY DAVID THOREAU

WE GET IN TROUBLE BY FOCUSING ON THINGS OVER WHICH WE HAVE NO CONTROL — WILL THIS MEETING GO OKAY, WILL MY CHILD GET WELL, WILL THAT PERSON LIKE ME, ETC. STOP IT! INSTEAD, FOCUS ON WHAT YOU CAN CONTROL — YOUR ATTITUDES, THOUGHTS, AND RESPONSIBILITIES.

IF YOU ARE GOING TO SUCCEED IN LIFE
YOU MUST WORK.
THERE IS NO SHORTCUT.

DID YOU KNOW?

Gary Player won more international golf tournaments in his day than anyone else. Today, he's still winning on the Seniors tour — and winning big.

One day he heard the comment, "I'd give anything if I could hit the ball just like you."

His response was, "No you wouldn't. You'd give anything to hit a golf ball like me if it was easy. You know what you've got to do to hit a golf ball like me? You've got to get up at five o'clock in the morning every day, go out on the course, and hit one thousand golf balls. Your hand starts bleeding, you walk up to the clubhouse, wash the blood off your hand, slap a bandage on it, and go out and hit another one thousand golf balls. That's what it takes to hit a golf ball like me."

DID YOU KNOW?

- You beat 50% of the people in America by working hard.

- You beat 40% by being a person of honesty and integrity and standing for something.

- And the last 10% is a dog fight in the free enterprise system.

  Art Williams

SUCCESS IS A MATTER OF
UNDERSTANDING AND RIGOROUSLY
PRACTICING SPECIFIC, SIMPLE HABITS.

— ROBERT RINGER

DID YOU KNOW?

- A successful year is the sum of successful months.

- A successful month is the sum of successful weeks.

- A successful week is the sum of successful days.

- A successful day is the sum of successful hours.

- A successful hour is the sum of successful habits.

WE ARE WHAT WE REPEATEDLY DO.

— ARISTOTLE

DISCIPLINE YOURSELF FOR THE PURPOSE OF GODLINESS.

— 1 TIMOTHY 4:7 NASB

Achieve personal significance.

I will live my life with
a sense of destiny.

WHAT YOU SEE, IS WHAT YOU'LL BE!

— JOHN MAXWELL

GOD DON'T MAKE NO JUNK!

— ETHEL WATERS

"FOR I KNOW THE PLANS I HAVE FOR YOU," DECLARES THE LORD, "PLANS TO PROSPER YOU AND NOT TO HARM YOU, PLANS TO GIVE YOU HOPE AND A FUTURE."

— *JEREMIAH 29:11*

DO YOU REALLY WANT TO GROW?
THEN SAY THIS TO A CLOSE FRIEND...
   "HERE ARE FIVE QUESTIONS I HOPE NO
   ONE EVER ASKS ME."
   THEN STATE YOUR QUESTIONS AND
   TELL YOUR FRIEND,
   "ONCE A WEEK, PLEASE ASK ME
   THOSE QUESTIONS."

DON'T PRETEND TO BE PERFECT, BUT PROGRESS. THAT IS THE KEY TO SUCCESS.

WALK IN THE LIGHT, AS HE IS IN THE LIGHT.

— 1 JOHN 1:7

YOU ARE GOING TO MAKE MISTAKES. IN FACT, YOU ARE GOING TO FAIL REPEATEDLY. JUST REMEMBER, FAILING DOESN'T MAKE A FAILURE. A TRUE FAILURE IS A PERSON WHO DOESN'T LEARN FROM HIS FAILURES.

LEARN TO FAIL FORWARD!

DO YOU WANT TO BE FREE? THEN
ADMIT YOUR MISTAKES TO YOURSELF,
OTHERS, AND GOD.

FILL IN THE SPACES BELOW:
I AM SPECIAL BECAUSE...

_____

_____

_____

_____

_____

FILL IN THE SPACES BELOW:
I NEED TO WORK ON THE
FOLLOWING AREAS...

_____

_____

_____

_____

_____

THE AVERAGE PERSON GOES TO HIS
GRAVE WITH HIS MUSIC STILL IN HIM.

— OLIVER WENDELL HOLMES

X OUT THE NEGATIVES.

I WILL EMBRACE PROBLEMS AS
POSITIVE OPPORTUNITIES.

OUR DOUBTS ARE TRAITORS AND MAKE
US LOSE THE GOOD WE OFT MIGHT WIN
BY FEARING TO ATTEMPT.

— SHAKESPEARE

FEAR IS THE DARKROOM WHERE
NEGATIVES ARE DEVELOPED.

— ZIG ZIGLAR

CRISIS CREATES OPPORTUNITY.

— CHINESE PROVERB

TO LIVE WITHOUT PAIN IS A MYTH.... IT IS TO BE HALF ALIVE. MANY OF US DO NOT REALIZE THAT PAIN AND JOY RUN TOGETHER. WHEN WE CUT OURSELVES OFF FROM PAIN, WE HAVE UNWITTINGLY CUT OURSELVES OFF FROM JOY AS WELL.

— CLYDE REID

THE FACT IS THAT LIFE IS EITHER
HARD AND SATISFYING OR
EASY AND UNSATISFYING.

— RICHARD LEIDER

THE ONLY CURE FOR SUFFERING IS TO
FACE IT HEAD ON, GRASP IT AROUND
THE NECK, AND USE IT.

— MARY CRAIG

IF YOU KEEP SAYING THAT THINGS ARE GOING TO BE BAD, YOU HAVE A GOOD CHANCE TO BE A PROPHET.

— ISAAC BASHEVIS SINGER

ALWAYS BE A CRITICAL THINKER.
ALWAYS HAVE A POSITIVE ATTITUDE!

THE ABC'S OF POSITIVE THINKING

- Accept problems.

- Believe the best.

- Cast off the negatives.

THINK OF THE THREE WORST FAILURES
IN YOUR LIFE AND WRITE THEM
DOWN HERE:

_____

_____

_____

NOW, CIRCLE THE WORST FAILURE, AND
THEN WRITE THREE POSITIVE THINGS
YOU LEARNED AS A RESULT OF IT.

_____

_____

_____

HOW DO YOU HANDLE PROBLEMS?
DO YOU *REACT* OR *RESPOND* TO THEM?
DO YOU GET *BITTER* OR *BETTER*?

DO YOU KNOW HOW TO TURN
PROBLEMS INTO POSSIBILITIES?

FACING PROBLEMS + CHOOSING JOY
= PATIENCE

PATIENCE + TIME × REPETITION
= FULFILLMENT

IF YOU HAVE TO GO MORE THAN THREE FEET FROM WHERE YOU ARE TO FIND FULFILLMENT, SOMETHING IS WRONG.

HOW ALIVE ARE YOU? ANSWER THESE QUESTIONS:

- **Have you wept at anything this past year?**

- **Have you thought seriously about the fact that you're going to die someday?**

- **Do you really listen when people are speaking to you, or are you just waiting for your turn to speak?**

- **Do you know anyone you would be willing to suffer great pain for, or even die for?**

Frederick Buechner

UNRESTRICTED WATER IS A SWAMP;
BECAUSE IT LACKS RESTRICTION,
IT ALSO LACKS DEPTH.

— TIM HANSEL

IF YOU WANT THE DEPTH OF POWER,
FREEDOM, AND CLARITY IN YOUR LIFE,
LEARN TO LIVE WITH YOUR LIMITATIONS
AND EMBRACE THEM.

THE KEY TO POSITIVE EMOTIONS, IS
POSITIVE, ACCURATE THINKING.

— DAVID BURNS

HE WHO LAUGHS, LASTS!

— ZIG ZIGLAR

INTERNALIZE RIGHT PRINCIPLES.

I WILL CENTER MY LIFE ON
BEDROCK PRINCIPLES.

YOU NEVER KNOW A LINE IS CROOKED
UNLESS YOU HAVE A STRAIGHT ONE TO
PUT NEXT TO IT.

— SOCRATES

IT IS HARD TO EXPECT AN EMPTY BAG
TO STAND UP STRAIGHT.

— WINSTON CHURCHILL

THE KEYS TO DOING WHAT IS RIGHT:

- Verify your own values.

- Articulate your own ethical grid and philosophy of life.

- Learn the proper perspectives on issues.

- Unpack right values through action.

- Evaluate your growth.

- Share these truths (your values) with other people.

WE CAN'T EXPECT OUR KIDS TO DO WHAT WE *TELL THEM*, IF WHAT WE'RE *SHOWING THEM* MEANS NOTHING.

WHAT MOSES BROUGHT DOWN FROM
MOUNT SINAI WERE NOT THE TEN
SUGGESTIONS — THEY ARE
COMMANDMENTS. ARE, NOT WERE.

DID YOU KNOW?

- Thirteen percent of the populace believes in the biblical Ten Commandments.

- Nine out of ten Americans lie regularly.

- One-fifth of the nation's children lose their virginity by age 13.

- For $10 million, seven percent of Americans would kill a stranger.

- A third of all AIDS carriers have not told their spouses or lovers.

YOU MUST IDENTIFY AND PROMOTE
THE VALUES YOU WANT TO
CHARACTERIZE YOURSELF. OR, YOU CAN
EXPECT TO SPEND THE REST OF YOUR
LIFE AS A SLAVE TO OTHER PEOPLE'S
VALUES, YOUR OWN DYSFUNCTIONS,
CULTURAL PRESSURES, OR THE VALUES
YOUR OWN BAD HABITS PRODUCE. THE
CHOICE IS YOURS.

KNOWLEDGE. I WILL FILL MY MIND WITH WORTHY THOUGHTS BY OBSERVING THE BEAUTIFUL WORLD AROUND ME, BY READING THE BEST BOOKS, AND BY ASSOCIATING WITH THE BEST COMPANIONS.

LEADERSHIP. I WILL MAKE MY INFLUENCE COUNT ON THE SIDE OF RIGHT, AVOIDING HABITS THAT WEAKEN AND DESTROY.

THESE THINGS I WILL DO NOW THAT I MAY BE WORTHY OF THE HIGH OFFICE OF TEACHER.

THERE IS HARMONY AND INNER PEACE
TO BE FOUND IN FOLLOWING A MORAL
COMPASS THAT POINTS IN THE SAME
DIRECTION, REGARDLESS OF FASHION
OR TREND.

— TED KOPPEL

ON MY HONOR, I WILL DO MY BEST:
TO DO MY DUTY TO GOD AND MY
COUNTRY, AND TO OBEY THE

SCOUT LAW:
TO HELP OTHER PEOPLE AT ALL TIMES;
TO KEEP MYSELF PHYSICALLY
STRONG, MENTALLY AWAKE, AND
MORALLY STRAIGHT.

— BOY SCOUT OATH

WHAT IS YOUR CODE OF CONDUCT?

_____

_____

_____

_____

_____

_____

_____

TAKE AN AUDIT OF YOUR VALUES BY ANSWERING THESE QUESTIONS:

- How do I spend my discretionary time?

- How do I spend my discretionary money?

- Who are my heroes?

- When I'm alone, what do I think about most?

WISDOM IS THE PRINCIPLE THING;
THEREFORE GET WISDOM:
AND WITH ALL THY GETTING GET
UNDERSTANDING. EXALT HER, AND SHE
SHALL PROMOTE THEE: SHE SHALL BRING
THEE TO HONOUR, WHEN THOU DOST
EMBRACE HER.

— PROVERBS 4:7,8 NKJV

MARCH TO A MISSION.

I WILL PASSIONATELY PURSUE MY MISSION.

WHAT DOES "MARCH TO A MISSION" MEAN?

It means living with a sense of destiny, passion, excitement, and meaning. It means knowing that you are living your life in a significant way.

THIS IS THE TRUE JOY IN LIFE....THE BEING
THOROUGHLY WORN OUT BEFORE YOU ARE
THROWN ON THE SCRAP HEAP. THE BEING A
FORCE OF NATURE INSTEAD OF A FEVERISH, SELFISH,
LITTLE CLOD OF AILMENTS.

— GEORGE BERNARD SHAW

WHAT LIES BEHIND US AND WHAT LIES BEFORE US
ARE TINY MATTERS COMPARED TO WHAT LIES
WITHIN US.

— OLIVER WENDELL HOLMES

DO YOU HAVE STRATEGIC GOALS? EACH ONE A·I·M·S.

- Is it **Achievable**?

- Is it **Inspiring**?

- Is it **Measurable**?

- Is it **Shared with others**?

THE WAY TO HAVE A LIFE OF IMPACT LIES WITHIN YOU — YOUR CHARACTER, THE VALUES AND PRINCIPLES THAT MOTIVATE YOU, THE WORTHINESS OF YOUR GOALS, THE TRUTH OF YOUR ABILITIES AND TALENTS. THESE ARE THE THINGS THAT GOVERN SUCCESS AND FAILURE IN YOUR LIFE.

DO YOU MARCH TO A MISSION?

- Do you have a clear picture of where you're going?

- Do others know about your plans?

- Have you set targets for your life?

- Do those you count on for support know about these targets?

- Are you satisfied with the targets you've set in your professional life?

- Are you satisfied with the targets you've set in your personal life?

- Do you have a written method to track your progress?

- Are your values clear and sharp in your mind?

- Have you written down the values you cherish?

- Do you ever feel guilty about success?

- Are you as successful as you can be?
  Richard Leider

FOCUS PRODUCES VELOCITY.

IF A MAN HAS A "WHY" FOR LIVING HE CAN STAND ANY "HOW."

— DAVID RAE

MORE AND MORE PEOPLE TODAY HAVE THE MEANS TO LIVE BUT NO MEANING TO LIVE FOR.

— VIKTOR FRANKL

ASK YOURSELF THESE QUESTIONS:

- How do I want myself to be different?

- How do I want my family to be different?

- How do I want my business to be different?

- How do I want my relationships to be different?

- How do I want my community to be different?

- How do I want the world to be different?

DEVELOP A DEEP SENSE OF THE
PRECIOUSNESS AND SHORTNESS OF
YOUR LIFE. AND LIVE IN LIGHT OF THAT!
WHATEVER YOU CAN DO, OR DREAM
YOU CAN DO, BEGIN IT. BOLDNESS HAS
GENIUS, POWER AND MAGIC IN IT.

— GOETHE

VISUALIZE YOURSELF SITTING IN A ROCKING CHAIR ON A BEAUTIFUL AUTUMN AFTERNOON. YOU ARE 90 YEARS OLD AND HAVE LIVED THE MOST PRODUCTIVE AND POSITIVE LIFE YOU CAN IMAGINE.

WHAT DOES IT LOOK LIKE? WHAT IS TRUE OF YOUR PERSONAL LIFE, MARRIAGE, FAMILY, BUSINESS IMPACT, COMMUNITY INFLUENCE, FINANCES, FRIENDS, ETC.?

WRITE DOWN THIS IDEAL SCENARIO.

IF A MAN HASN'T DISCOVERED
SOMETHING HE WILL DIE FOR,
HE ISN'T FIT TO LIVE.

— MARTIN LUTHER KING, JR.

INTEGRATE ALL OF LIFE.

I WILL KEEP ALL VITAL AREAS
OF MY LIFE IN BALANCE.

DID YOU KNOW?

Your top three daily priorities should be:

1) Love God.

2) Love yourself (take care of yourself mentally, physically, emotionally).

3) Love others (at home, work, community, church).

*LOVE THE LORD YOUR GOD WITH ALL
YOUR HEART AND WITH ALL YOUR SOUL
AND WITH ALL YOUR STRENGTH AND
WITH ALL YOUR MIND; AND LOVE YOUR
NEIGHBOR AS YOURSELF.*

— JESUS CHRIST
LUKE 10:27

Life Maximizers

IF I HAD MY LIFE TO LIVE OVER AGAIN, I WOULD DARE TO MAKE
MORE MISTAKES NEXT TIME. I WOULD RELAX. I WOULD BE SILLIER.
I WOULD TAKE FEWER THINGS SERIOUSLY.... I WOULD EAT MORE
ICE CREAM AND LESS BEANS. I WOULD PERHAPS HAVE MORE
ACTUAL TROUBLES BUT FEWER IMAGINARY ONES. YOU SEE, I'M
ONE OF THOSE PEOPLE WHO LIVED SERIOUSLY AND SANELY
HOUR AFTER HOUR, DAY AFTER DAY. I'VE BEEN ONE OF THOSE
PERSONS WHO NEVER WENT ANYPLACE WITHOUT A
THERMOMETER, A HOT WATER BOTTLE, A RAINCOAT,
AND A PARACHUTE. IF I HAD TO DO IT OVER AGAIN,
I'D TRAVEL LIGHTER.

— EIGHTY-FIVE-YEAR-OLD WOMAN FROM
THE HILL COUNTRY OF KENTUCKY

WHAT DOES A MAN GET FOR ALL THE TOIL AND ANXIOUS STRIVING WITH WHICH HE LABORS UNDER THE SUN? ALL HIS DAYS HIS WORK IS PAIN AND GRIEF; EVEN AT NIGHT HIS MIND DOES NOT REST. THIS TOO IS MEANINGLESS.

— KING SOLOMON
  ECCLESIATES 2:22, 23

Life Maximizers

WHAT IS LIFE ABOUT? IT IS NOT ABOUT WRITING GREAT BOOKS,
AMASSING GREAT WEALTH, ACHIEVING GREAT POWER. IT IS
ABOUT LOVING AND BEING LOVED. IT IS ABOUT ENJOYING
YOUR FOOD AND SITTING IN THE SUN RATHER THAN RUSHING
THROUGH LUNCH AND HURRYING BACK TO THE OFFICE. IT IS
ABOUT SAVORING THE BEAUTY OF THE MOMENTS THAT
DON'T LAST: THE SUNSETS, THE LEAVES TURNING COLOR, THE
RARE MOMENTS OF TRUE COMMUNICATION. IT IS ABOUT
SAVORING THEM RATHER THAN MISSING OUT ON THEM
BECAUSE WE ARE SO BUSY. THEY WILL NOT HOLD STILL UNTIL WE
GET AROUND TO THEM.

— HAROLD KUSHNER

WHEN WORK STARTS TO BECOME A GOD
IN OUR LIVES WE'RE IN TROUBLE. I WANT
YOU TO SUCCEED IN YOUR WORK, BUT
YOU CAN'T LET ANYTHING MATERIAL
BECOME YOUR GOD. IF YOU DO YOU'LL
LOSE BALANCE IN THE OTHER AREAS OF
YOUR LIFE.

BURNOUT IS WHEN A "JOB IS A JOB IS A JOB."

ONLY TO THE EXTENT THAT WE CAN
MANAGE OUR PERSONAL LIVES AND OUR
FAMILIES CAN WE SUCCESSFULLY MANAGE
IN THE PUBLIC ARENA.

*NOW THE OVERSEER MUST BE ABOVE
REPROACH....HE MUST MANAGE HIS
OWN FAMILY WELL.*

— *I TIMOTHY 3:2,4*

THINK OF *BALANCE* IN TERMS OF A
MARBLE AND A ROUNDED BOWL. STATIC
EQUILIBRIUM IS WHEN THE MARBLE JUST
SITS AT THE BOTTOM OF THE BOWL.
TURN THE BOWL OVER ON ITS LIP.
DYNAMIC EQUILIBRIUM IS WHEN YOU
KEEP THE MARBLE ON THE TOP.
CONSTANT ADJUSTMENT IS NEEDED.

LET YOUR PRIORITIES DETERMINE
YOUR SCHEDULE.

DON'T LET YOUR SCHEDULE DETERMINE
YOUR PRIORITIES.

ARE YOU FLEXIBLE? TRY THIS:

Be very aware of your circumstances and the people around you, listen actively and empathically, be thankful when an interruption enters your life, and embrace every experience as a meaningful and ordained opportunity to grow, develop, and become all that you need to become.

EIGHTY-FIVE PERCENT OF ALL EMPLOYEES
WHO ARE FIRED ARE LET GO BECAUSE OF
RELATIONAL CONFLICT OR LACK OF
RELATIONAL SKILLS, NOT LACK OF
TECHNICAL SKILLS.

LOVE PEOPLE AND USE THINGS,
NOT VICE VERSA.

SUCCESS IS NOT JUST THE END RESULT, BUT THE PROCESS OF ACHIEVING IT AS WELL. IN FACT, THE DEGREE OF SUCCESS IN THE PRODUCT OF OUR LIVES IS IN DIRECT PROPORTION TO THE DEGREE OF SUCCESS WE HAVE IN THE PROCESS.

LIFE IS LIKE JUGGLING CRYSTAL BALLS AND
RUBBER BALLS; SUCCESS DEPENDS ON
KNOWING WHICH IS WHICH.

— ROY ROBERTS

ZERO IN ON CARING FOR PEOPLE.

I WILL PUT OTHERS FIRST AND
HONESTLY SERVE THEM.

A SERVANT LEADER IS ONE WHO GETS
EXCITED ABOUT MAKING OTHER PEOPLE
MORE SUCCESSFUL THAN HIMSELF.

AUTHENTIC SUCCESS INVOLVES TAKING
RESPONSIBILITY TO CARE, KNOWING
THAT PART OF YOUR "CALLING" OR
"MISSION" ON THIS EARTH IS TO
POSITIVELY TOUCH OTHERS AND TO
CARE FOR THEM. THIS IS NOT JUST THE
JOB OF THE SOCIAL WORKER, RABBI,
PASTOR, OR PSYCHOLOGIST.
IT'S YOUR JOB.

THE AVERAGE PARENT MAKES 10
NEGATIVE STATEMENTS TO EVERY 1
POSITIVE STATEMENT TO THEIR CHILD.

— AMERICAN INSTITUTE OF FAMILY RELATIONS

IT TAKES 4 POSITIVE STATEMENTS TO
OVERCOME 1 NEGATIVE STATEMENT.

HOW DO YOU RESPOND WHEN PEOPLE
FAIL AROUND YOU?

DO YOU GIVE UP ON THEM OR
EXPRESS SHAME?

OR, DO YOU BELIEVE IN THEM?

SYMPATHY IS WHEN SOMEONE HITS HIS THUMB WITH A HAMMER AND YOU SAY, "OH, I'M SO SORRY." EMPATHY IS WHEN SOMEONE HITS HIS THUMB WITH A HAMMER AND YOU SAY, "OUCH!" YOU FEEL WITH THE OTHER PERSON.

OTHER PEOPLE NEED YOU;
YOU NEED OTHER PEOPLE!

THE HINGES ON THE DOOR TO
INTIMATE, UNIFIED RELATIONSHIPS
ARE GREASED BY THE LEVEL OF
TRUST YOU HAVE IN AND WITH
THOSE AROUND YOU.

TEAM UNITY IS...

- Giving up my own agenda to develop a better one.

- Combining my uniqueness with another person or a group of people, to create something new.

- Choosing to be more excited about the success of the team (or the other person) than that of myself.

- A spirit of oneness where I seek to build up those around me and be open and honest in the process.

HOW DO YOU BUILD TEAM UNITY?

- Uplift one another.

- Need one another.

- Intimately relate to one another.

- Trust one another.

- Yield to one another.

THE BIGGEST DISEASE TODAY IS NOT LEPROSY OR TUBERCULOSIS, BUT RATHER THE FEELING OF BEING UNWANTED, UNCARED FOR, AND DESERTED BY EVERYBODY.

— MOTHER TERESA

IT IS ONLY BY RISKING OUR PERSONS
FROM ONE HOUR TO THE NEXT THAT
WE LIVE AT ALL.

— WILLIAM JAMES

CONTINUAL FIGHTING PRODUCES ONLY
BRUISES, BREAKS, AND RESISTANT PEOPLE.
BUT WHEN YOU LEARN TO YIELD
APPROPRIATELY, AT THE RIGHT TIME,
YOU'LL TAKE ALL THE HOT AIR OUT OF
AN ARGUMENT AND ALLOW OTHERS TO
RESPOND POSITIVELY.

THINK ABOUT WHAT MESSAGE YOU CONVEY TO YOUR SPOUSE AND CHILDREN IF YOU YIELD.

When You Say...	Your Family Hears...
"Honey, I apologize, you were right."	Humility and openness to talk.
"I'll try to be home at 6:00, four days a week."	Flexibility, caring for your children and spouse.
"What would you like me to do?"	Honoring family before seeking advice.

A FRIEND IS SOMEONE WHO KNOWS
ALL ABOUT ME, LIKES ME FOR
WHO I AM AND HAS NO PLANS FOR
MY PERSONAL IMPROVEMENT.

AS IRON SHARPENS IRON, SO ONE MAN SHARPENS ANOTHER.

— *PROVERBS 27:17*

IF YOUR ENEMY IS NEEDY, MEET THAT
NEED. THAT WILL TAKE ALL OF THE WIND
OUT OF HIS SAILS. BUT IF YOU FIGHT
HIM, HE WILL FIGHT BACK AND HIS SPIRIT
WILL CLOSE.

DYING TO YOURSELF ENSURES GROWTH IN OTHERS. THIS IS TRUE OF GREAT MOTHERS, EFFECTIVE EXECUTIVES, WINNING PROFESSIONALS, AND SUCCESSFUL EMPLOYEES. AS WE GROW IN HUMILITY, THOSE AROUND US OPEN UP TO CHANGE, AND WE GROW AS WELL.

PUTTING OTHERS FIRST IS A SIGN OF
CHARACTER, NOT COMPROMISE.

— MARY JENSON

ENERGIZE INNER LIFE.

I WILL CULTIVATE MY CHARACTER
AND SPIRIT.

CHARACTER IS WHAT YOU ARE
IN THE DARK.

— D.L. MOODY

THE LORD DOES NOT LOOK AT THE
THINGS MAN LOOKS AT. MAN LOOKS AT
THE OUTWARD APPEARANCE, BUT THE
LORD LOOKS AT THE HEART.

— I SAMUEL 16:7

NEARLY ALL MEN CAN STAND ADVERSITY,
BUT IF YOU WANT TO TEST A MAN'S
CHARACTER, GIVE HIM POWER.

— ABRAHAM LINCOLN

I HAVE CONQUERED AN EMPIRE,
BUT I HAVE NOT BEEN ABLE
TO CONQUER MYSELF.

— PETER THE GREAT

PEOPLE GROW THROUGH EXPERIENCE IF
THEY MEET LIFE HONESTLY AND
COURAGEOUSLY. THIS IS HOW
CHARACTER IS BUILT.

— ELEANOR ROOSEVELT

HISTORY CARES NOT AN IOTA FOR
THE RANK OR TITLE A MAN HAS BORNE,
BUT ONLY THE QUALITY OF HIS DEEDS
AND THE CHARACTER OF HIS MIND
AND HEART.

— SAMUEL LOGAN BRENGLE

DID YOU KNOW?

If you...

- Sow an act, you reap a habit.

- Sow a habit, you reap a character.

- Sow a character, you reap a destiny.

Charles Reade

CHARACTER IS NOT MADE IN A CRISIS —
IT IS ONLY EXHIBITED.

— ROBERT FREEMAN

THE ONLY ASSURANCE OF OUR NATION'S
SAFETY IS TO LAY OUR FOUNDATION IN
MORALITY AND RELIGION.

— ABRAHAM LINCOLN

IF GOD DOES NOT EXIST,
EVERYTHING IS PERMISSIBLE.

— DOSTOYEVSKY

CHARACTER-CENTEREDNESS FLOWING
FROM SPIRITUAL ROOTS IS THE
ULTIMATE SOURCE OF OUR POWER
INDIVIDUALLY, INSTITUTIONALLY,
AND SOCIETALLY.

SURVEY AFTER SURVEY REVEALS THAT
RELIGIOUS PEOPLE, MORE OFTEN THAN
NONRELIGIOUS PEOPLE, REPORT FEELING
HAPPY AND SATISFIED WITH LIFE.

— DR. DAVID MYERS

TO BE WHAT IS CALLED HAPPY, ONE SHOULD HAVE :

- something to live on;

- something to live for;

- something to die for.

Cyprian Norwid

CULTIVATING SPIRITUALITY IS BUILDING A SIGNIFICANT AND MEANINGFUL RELATIONSHIP WITH A PERSONAL GOD.

BE STILL, AND KNOW THAT I AM GOD.

— PSALM 46:10

FOCUS ON CHARACTER, NOT PERFORMANCE.

FOCUS ON RELATIONSHIP WITH GOD, NOT
   JUST FOLLOWING RULES.

FOCUS ON PROGRESSING, NOT PRETENDING
   TO BE PERFECT.

FOCUS ON OPENNESS AND HONESTY, NOT
   DENYING OR HIDING YOUR FAULTS.

WE ARE NOT HUMAN BEINGS HAVING A SPIRITUAL EXPERIENCE. WE ARE SPIRITUAL BEINGS HAVING A HUMAN EXPERIENCE.

— WAYNE DYERS

I HAVE SO MUCH TO DO TODAY THAT I MUST SPEND THREE HOURS IN PRAYER AND MEDITATION TO GET IT ALL DONE.

— MARTIN LUTHER

THE CAPACITY TO BECOME ENTHUSED
IS A SPIRITUAL QUALITY GENERATED
FROM WITHIN; IT DOESN'T NEED PEP
TALKS OR PERKS....I AM VALUABLE
BECAUSE GOD CREATED ME WITH
INNER VALUE AND WORTH.

— DENIS WAITLEY

FAITH IS BELIEVING THAT POSITIVE THINGS CAN COME OUT OF WHEREVER YOU ARE IN YOUR LIFE. HOWEVER, FAITH IS ONLY AS GOOD AS THE OBJECT IN WHICH IT IS PLACED. THE EFFECTIVENESS OF YOUR FAITH IS IN DIRECT PROPORTION TO YOUR SENSE OF THE REALITY OF A LIVING GOD.

FAITH IS LIKE A MUSCLE — THE MORE YOU USE IT THE STRONGER AND BIGGER IT GROWS.

TRY PRAYING BY PRACTICING:

- **Adoration** — praising God.

- **Confession** — admit your weaknesses and sins.

- **Thanksgiving** — thank God for specific things.

- **Supplication** — tell God your needs.

REAL POWER IS WHO YOU ARE AT YOUR CORE.
IT'S YOUR INNER MAN. IT'S YOUR DEPTH OF
FAITH. IT'S YOUR SPIRITUAL VIRILITY. THAT'S
THE REAL SOURCE OF ULTIMATE POWER.

YOUR INNER MAN IS YOUR TAPROOT. THIS
TAPROOT IS THE "MAIN ROOT OF A PLANT,
USUALLY STOUTER THAN THE LATERAL ROOTS
AND GROWING STRAIGHT DOWNWARD
FROM THE STEM." WITHOUT IT THE REST WILL
QUICKLY ROT AND DIE.

*NOW ALL HAS BEEN HEARD; HERE IS THE
CONCLUSION OF THE MATTER: FEAR GOD
AND KEEP HIS COMMANDMENTS, FOR THIS
IS THE WHOLE DUTY OF MAN. FOR GOD
WILL BRING EVERY DEED INTO JUDGMENT,
INCLUDING EVERY HIDDEN THING,
WHETHER IT IS GOOD OR EVIL.*

— KING SOLOMON
ECCLESIASTES 12:13,14

AMERICA IS GREAT BECAUSE AMERICA IS GOOD; IF SHE EVER CEASES TO BE GOOD, SHE WILL CEASE TO BE GREAT.

— ALEXIS DE TOCQUEVILLE

Revise actions rigorously.

I will keep adjusting to needs.

IF YOU WANT TO DOUBLE YOUR
SUCCESS RATIO, DOUBLE YOUR
FAILURE RATE.

— HARVEY MACKAY

MISTAKES HAPPEN ALL THE TIME. EVERY
TIME YOU MAKE A MISTAKE AND LEARN
FROM IT, YOU BUILD STRENGTH
AND CHARACTER.

— HARVEY MACKAY

DO YOU HAVE:

- A personal mentor or counselor,

- A spiritual counselor,

- A resource person,

- A practical friend?

INVITE YOUR FRIENDS AND COLLEAGUES
TO POINT OUT ANYTHING IN YOUR LIFE
THAT NEEDS TO CHANGE. LET THEM
INVADE YOUR LIFE AND SHOW YOU
WHEN THERE'S SOME MISTAKE YOU
MIGHT BE MAKING CONSISTENTLY.

THERE IS NOTHING PERMANENT
EXCEPT CHANGE.

— HERACLITUS

TO LIVE IS TO CHANGE, AND TO BE
PERFECT IS TO HAVE CHANGED OFTEN.

— JOHN HENRY NEWMAN

FOR A CONSCIOUS BEING, TO EXIST IS TO CHANGE, TO CHANGE IS TO MATURE, TO MATURE IS TO GO ON CREATING ONESELF ENDLESSLY.

— HENRI BERGSON

EVERYTHING THAT CAN BE INVENTED
HAS ALREADY BEEN INVENTED.

— CHARLES H. DUELL, HEAD OF THE U.S. PATENT
OFFICE AT THE TURN OF THE 20TH CENTURY

THE MOST SUCCESSFUL PERSON IS
USUALLY THE ONE WITH THE
BEST INFORMATION.

HOW TO SCREEN INFORMATION:

- Know what is important to know.

- Understand what is meant by the information.

- Decide what to do with the data.

LASER-LIKE FOCUS IS PERHAPS THE
MOST COMMON TRADEMARK OF THE
SUPER-SUCCESSFUL.

— ROBERT RINGER

THAT WHICH HOLDS OUR ATTENTION
DETERMINES OUR ACTION.

— WILLIAMS JAMES

BE WARNED: THERE IS NO END OF OPINIONS READY TO BE EXPRESSED. STUDYING THEM CAN GO ON FOREVER, AND BECOME VERY EXHAUSTING!

— *ECCLESIASTES 12:12 TLB*

STAY THE COURSE.

I WILL NEVER, EVER, EVER QUIT.

- **Colonel Sanders built the Kentucky Fried Chicken empire. However, he was rejected 1,009 times before someone accepted his ideas.**

- **Ty Cobb was a world class baseball player, but he was thrown out of games for stealing bases more times than anyone in baseball's history.**

- **Babe Ruth struck out more times than 99 percent of major league players.**

- Enrico Caruso's voice teacher told him to quit singing.

- Thomas Edison's teacher called him a dunce.

- It took Edison 14,000 failures to perfect the light bulb.

- What do you want to make of your life?

THERE IS NO POVERTY THAT CAN
OVERTAKE DILIGENCE.

— JAPANESE PROVERB

BY PERSEVERANCE THE SNAIL
REACHED THE ARK.

— CHARLES SPURGEON

CONSIDER THESE FINDINGS FROM THE NATIONAL SALES EXECUTIVES ASSOCIATION CONCERNING SALES PERSISTENCE:

- 80% of all new sales are made after the fifth call to the same prospect.

- 48% of all sales persons make one call, then cross off the prospect.

- 25% percent quit after the second call.

- 12% of all sales representatives call three times, then quit.

- 10% keep calling until they succeed.

YOU MEASURE THE SIZE OF AN ACCOMPLISHMENT BY THE OBSTACLES YOU HAVE TO OVERCOME TO REACH YOUR GOALS.

— BOOKER T. WASHINGTON

WHEN WOULD YOU HAVE QUIT?

1831 — Failed in business

1832 — Defeated for legislature

1833 — Second failure in business

1836 — Suffered nervous breakdown

1838 — Defeated for speaker

1840 — Defeated for elector

1843 — Defeated for Congress

1848 — Defeated for Congress

1855 — Defeated for Senate

1856 — Defeated for Vice President

1858 — Defeated for Senate.

1860 — **ABRAHAM LINCOLN
ELECTED PRESIDENT**

OUR GREATEST MORAL PROBLEM TODAY
IS COWARDICE. IT'S COWARDICE THAT
PREVENTS US FROM COMING UP WITH
NEW THOUGHTS.

— WILLIAM SLOANE COFFIN, JR.

CONSIDER THE FOLLOWING QUIP ABOUT THE LIFE OF A POSTAGE STAMP:

- I represent my country.

- I am always ready for service.

- I go wherever I am sent.

- I do whatever I am asked to do.

- I stick to my task until it is done.

- I don't strike back when I am struck.

- I don't give up when I am licked.

- I am necessary to the happiness of the world.

- I keep up-to-date.

WHEN NOTHING SEEMS TO HELP, I GO AND
LOOK AT A STONECUTTER, HAMMERING
AWAY AT HIS ROCK, PERHAPS A HUNDRED
TIMES WITHOUT AS MUCH AS A CRACK
SHOWING IN IT. YET AT THE HUNDRED AND
FIRST BLOW IT WILL SPLIT IN TWO, AND I
KNOW IT WAS NOT THAT BLOW THAT DID IT
— BUT ALL THAT HAD GONE BEFORE.

— JACOB RIIS

ARE YOU:

- Faithful

- Loyal

- True

- Constant

- Steadfast

- Staunch

- Resolute

- Trustworthy?

OATH TAKEN BY THE YOUNG MEN OF ANCIENT ATHENS

We will never bring disgrace on this our City by an act of dishonesty or cowardice.

We will fight for the ideals and Sacred Things of the City both alone and with many.

We will revere and obey the City's laws, and will do our best to incite a like reverence and respect in those above us who are prone to annul them or set them at naught.

We will strive increasingly to quicken the public's sense of civic duty.

Thus in all these ways we will transmit this City, not only not less, but greater and more beautiful than it was transmitted to us.

FOR EVERYONE, SURELY, WHAT WE HAVE GONE THROUGH IN THIS PERIOD...THIS IS THE LESSON: NEVER GIVE IN, NEVER GIVE IN, NEVER, NEVER, NEVER, NEVER — NOTHING GREAT OR SMALL, LARGE OR PETTY — NEVER GIVE IN EXCEPT TO CONVICTIONS OF HONOR AND GOOD SENSE. NEVER YIELD TO FORCE; NEVER YIELD TO THE APPARENTLY OVERWHELMING MIGHT OF THE ENEMY.

    — WINSTON CHURCHILL

HOW WILL YOU BE REMEMBERED WHEN YOU DIE? WHAT WILL PEOPLE BE SAYING AT YOUR FUNERAL? I ASK THESE QUESTIONS TO SHOCK YOU INTO REFRAMING YOUR PERSPECTIVE.

IF YOU CHOOSE TO LIVE RIGHT AND ALIGN YOUR LIFE WITH TRUTH, YOU WILL LEAVE A VIVID, POSITIVE, AND POWERFUL LEGACY.

CONCLUSION

The Maximizer principles I have shared with you are not just
haphazard principles. They are intended to be a map — a model —
a way of looking at life.

I guarantee you that if you can build these principles into the fabric of
your being and let them be the roots for your understanding of life,
you will have the kind of perspective that will make you a success
in every sense of the word. You'll be the kind of significant
individual you truly want to be.

Can you truly leave a vital, significant legacy as you maximize your
days on this earth? I believe you can and you **must!**

ABOUT THE AUTHOR

Ron Jenson is an internationally known author, convention speaker, and executive coach. He is the chairman of Future Achievement, International, a company providing educational programs, products, and services for personal development; and High Ground, a worldwide association of leaders in business, government, academia, the professions, and entertainment committed to leadership education programs internationally. He holds a masters in education and doctorate in the area of leadership development.

Dr. Jenson and his wife, Mary, live in San Diego, California. They have two grown children, Matt and Molly.